# How to Be Happy and Live Life to the Fullest

## A Guide to Reaching Your Full Potential

### By: Kevin Kerr

2 How to Be Happy and Live Life to the Fullest

All is perfectly well, as it's always been, for all of eternity.

4 How to Be Happy and Live Life to the Fullest

## Copyright © 2015 by Kevin Kerr - All rights reserved.

In no way is it legal to reproduce, duplicate, or transmit any part of this document in either electronic means or in printed format. Recording of this publication is strictly prohibited and any storage of this document is not allowed unless with written permission from the publisher.

The information provided herein is stated to be truthful and consistent, in that any liability, in terms of inattention or otherwise, by any usage or abuse of any policies, processes, or directions contained within is the solitary and utter responsibility of the recipient reader. Under no circumstances will any legal responsibility or blame be held against the publisher for any reparation, damages, or monetary loss due to the information herein, either directly or indirectly.

The information herein is offered for informational purposes solely, and is universal as so. The presentation of the information is without contract or any type of guarantee assurance.

You should consult your physician or other health care professional before making any lifestyle or nutritional changes that are discussed, in order to determine if the suggested practices are right for your needs.

# Table of Contents

Introduction
Chapter 1.) Self Analysis
    Affirmations
    Relationships
    Making Changes
    Purpose
    Breathing
Chapter 2.) Enlightenment is the Way
    Acceptance
    Meditation
    Letting Go
    Silence
Chapter 3.) Manifesting Your Desires
    Intentions
    Desires
    Goals
    Sexual Energy
Chapter 4.) Feel Good All the Time
    Water
    Food
    Fasting
    Toxins
Summary

# Introduction

We can all agree that authentic happiness comes from within and does not stem from temporary outer circumstances. If you really want to feel at peace, then your goal is to let go of the ego which separates us from being at one with all which is. The majority of the population is so caught up in the past or future that they let the miracle and exquisite beauty of existence, which is always in the constant change of form, pass them by right now. However, reaching this inner awareness can be a difficult task or may have to be postponed till later on in life due to our responsibilities, goals, and all of the negative stimulus that we are surrounded with in today's day and age. The main reason people are not happy with their lives is because they aren't living a life of service to others that are truly in need, or they are even aware that they exist! Whatever it is you want to do, be, or feel the passion must be there for it to occur. The importance is of equal value in the universe whether your wish is to be an actor, a doctor, feel great all the time, be independent from society, get a job, establish a career, or wipe elderly butts in a nursing home. For a desire to become real it simply takes a strong will.

I'm here to teach you how to reach your full potential in this given moment, which will allow you to experience as well as manifest anything your heart desires. We must all understand that science and logic get us so far in regards to inner peace and physical well-being, then love for all that is takes us even further, and finally the soul will take you the rest of the way to peace from egoic mind. I'm going to show you how possible it is to create the life of your dreams as long as you first know exactly what it is you want. This is done by proper goal setting, merely feeling good, visualization, and a strong burning desire for the achievement. However, if you are not entirely willing to learn and entirely capable of accepting change then it will be more difficult to manifest what you want.

    If your aspiration is to feel and look your best then the willingness to make changes in your everyday routines and habits must first be present. You are the creator of your reality. If you're not happy with your life it's because you are letting your mind tell you that you are not happy. Your thoughts control your actions which in turn create the way you look and feel. If you want to alter your lifestyle for your benefit or accomplish something new it can only be done if you learn to let go of doubtful thoughts. This moment is perfect, and right now everything is possible. You can have anything and everything your heart desires!

## Chapter 1.) Self Analysis

  You can't change the world, but you can change how you feel about the world. In other words you cannot change society or the people in it, but you can change your world. Throughout life there is only going to be ups and downs if you let your mind attach itself to people or allow it claim things as its own. The ego is either your best friend or worst enemy. I have found it best to treat it as a child. Nurture them until they are strong enough to be on their own, and they both will be present in your life when the time is right. At the end of the day you are not your child as you are not your ego.

  Once we build up our emotional immune system, nothing that occurs in the outside world can harm the way we feel inside. Our ego likes to identify with everything around us which can cause pain when changes occur, but in reality we all belong to the universe and death is simply an illusion. The first step to creating your ideal life is to sort out everything that you do want and don't want. For example, if there are tasks throughout your day that bring you pain then it is important to wholeheartedly accept them or let go of everything that you don't enjoy be because it is our mission to love every second of our time here. If there is a relationship that is causing you to suffer then it is necessary to let go of it so that you can be free of the attachment or typically it is the other persons attachment which restricts your freedom. Anything we identify with, including our own physical body, causes us to be unhappy when our mind imagines us without it. In reality everything is perfectly whole and exactly how it needs to be. The mind is what separates us from experiencing the true beauty of life.

The number one key to happiness and reaching your full potential is to cultivate a life that you're excited about. Your life improves at the rate at which you forgive yourself and accept your current life circumstance because after all you created it. Before you can be accepting of the present, you must let go of everything from the past because it distracts your attention from what is in front of you right now. If you let go of all your pain from past experiences it manifests a focus within you that will bring whatever you desire. These principles have allowed me to live in the moment more and accept that nothing in life is either good or bad, because it just is what it is. What someone believes to be true is valid for them. For example, one might think potato chips taste wonderful and consider them to be a health food, the next person might believe they don't taste so well and may not agree. Neither person is right or wrong and is truly only subject to his or her own belief systems. The truths of one are valid for him or her but not the same as another. Since birth we have been accumulating mental programs that often slow us down from reaching our full potential. Another concept to be aware of is to not think of issues that arise in your life as problems, they should be thought of as opportunities to learn and better yourself. We must first learn to be more conscious of everything we think and do on a daily basis before we can truly master our minds and take complete control over our lives.

There are a lot of reasons why we can have racing thoughts that we do not enjoy. All come from what we have picked up from our environment but more specifically we lack control of our minds because a lack of adequate nutrition, a lack of sleep, certain television, music, not enough blood flow to the brain, trauma from our past, or an oxygen deficiency. Sometimes we cope with thoughts by using drugs, alcohol, tobacco, or over eating food in attempt to try to feel better which may temporarily work but it in turn will not get you closer to freeing yourself from the ego which is the root of the problem.

The ego cannot be treated as an enemy because it will only become stronger using this method, it must be treated with kindness. Nearly everyone on the planet has one, unless transcended, whether they want to admit it or believe it. One might believe that they cannot live without it, but the spirit knows what the body needs to live. Unlike the ego whereas it needs the body to survive. It is like our separate personality, or multiple personalities that associates things such as accomplishments, money, knowledge, material items, even the physical body, as the self, or more simplistically stated the ego is thoughts it has identified with the self. However, you are not your ego though; you are a special unique soul with unlimited power. The ego is a part of the mind that will generally argue with others to try to prove its beliefs right even though nothing can ever be truly be considered a fact because everything in life is someone's opinion and will always eventually be proven false with time. The ego is only present in our lives when we become lost in our own thoughts and become unconscious. Some of us have identified with thought patterns that are harming us, but we all have the power to change these to uplifting, beneficial words. Also, everyone has the power to free themselves of excessive thinking, but we must first recondition our normal thought patterns to our own specific desires which in turn will change our lives to whatever we think about. To rid your mind of thoughts you do not wish to have anymore, practice by accepting these patterns you do not enjoy. Next, you must strive to understand why you have them and eventually when they come into consciousness you will be mentally strong enough to dismiss them until they never come back. Sometimes we associate material items with the self as well. We can even feel physical pain when something we own is damaged. As I grow older I feel much better with less material items. Don't get me wrong I still enjoy having a few items but trust me a simple life is a more peaceful one.

    Physically everything you have ever seen, heard, touched, smelled, or tasted has created has created a path within the brain that neurons travel when events occur. The more often neurons travel these pathways; the more we get caught up with our same way of thinking. For example, when you spill something then it might signal you to get mad, or perhaps sad, but we don't have to feel any emotion when something of this nature occurs. If we always have a thought pattern such as, "bad things always happen to me", then we must stop having these thoughts and change it to, "good things always to happen to me." When you think "I'm mad" or "I'm sad" you should change these to "I'm glad". If you ever have the thought "I'm scared" then switch it to "I'm peared" or "I'm cared for", and go eat a pear. My guess is that you'll never have these thoughts again. When you think "I'm alone", you can simply change it to "I'm home". Another one that worked to replace two negative thought patterns for me was "I'm blessed" instead of "I'm stressed" or "I'm depressed. Get creative and eventually you can step back, witness your thoughts, and laugh at them as they pass through the mind.

You get what you think about most of the time; so if you continue to have thoughts of the things you do not want then you will continue to get those things until you change your thoughts. On a physical level when you are unconscious, which means to not be present with the moment or in your body, the ego is functioning by transmitting neurons through the most traveled neural pathways that our brain runs on. The ego is only useful until a certain point on our life and then it can be let go. It is always thinking about the future or caught up in the past which causes anxiety and stress.

Right now I want you to look at your hands and feel them... Feel each tip, each individual finger, or both hands wholly at the same time. Most have never intentionally been present within their body before so this can be a pleasant surprise and I am here to tell you it only gets better! The best way to free yourself from thoughts of stress and anxiety is to feel within the body, and the best places to start are the hands, feet, head, and stomach. If there is tension in your stomach then, like any pain, it will go away if you focus on it. Fasting can speed up the process of removing stomach tension if letting go does not take care of the problem, which I talk about more in chapter four. You have the power to feel however you want! You also have the ability to accomplish and experience anything you desire! If you enjoy this book, I believe it to be beneficial to keep rereading it until you master all of the mentioned concepts, ideas, and practices. The best way that we can improve self-control regarding our thoughts is by feeling within the body regularly because this takes us away from the mind. Practice makes perfect and the eventual goal is to feel the entire body at once, all of the day, which is the essence of enlightenment. After a while you will master this concept and you can always go back to being inside of your body whenever you need it. Try now to set still for a minute or two and be at one with your thoughts… If you have had no thoughts, or ones that you are at peace with, then you are on track! If not, it's okay and with time you will have complete control of your thoughts.

## Affirmations

For happiness to blossom one must be in a state of non-resistance. If you are not happy then it is most likely because your mind is focusing on the lack of things that it wants instead expressing gratitude of existence and for everything that is in front of it. A great way to become more at peace is to start by monitoring all your thoughts and looking for the ones that being with "I am...." The life you live shapes to the thoughts you have so it's wise to watch what comes after these two words. If you want to get a job, then it is the thoughts that keep you motivated as well as encouraged until the goal is achieved. Integrity is key for all aspects of your life. Once one masters this it will allow them to make decisions based on love and choices that support all of mankind.

There are two ways to be happy and at peace with your thoughts. One is to retrain your thoughts to be more loving, inspiring, and uplifting and the other is to stop having thoughts all together. The second can be difficult in today's day and age unless of course money and demanding priorities are not an issue. Now I want to show you techniques and methods to help you change your thoughts. The first obvious way is to think "I am happy" when "I am" surfaces into consciousness, but this is not always possible. Affirmations are an excellent effective way to reshape the thoughts that come into your mind. They are written positive statements that should be read every day, as often as your heart desires. I have used many different affirmations throughout my life, and I can attest that the more you reread them the more you will believe in yourself and the faster they will manifest into your reality. Your affirmations should be tailored to your wants and needs of the life your live right now. I can honestly say I would not be at the level of peace I am today without the use of affirmations.

    You can also include goals that you feel can be accomplished in the near future, but make sure they are written in a manner that it already has been accomplished so that it instills the belief in which it has already been done. For example, an affirmation pertaining to manifesting a job would be "I have my dream job" rather than "I want a job". They will work wonders in your life for anything that you might be having trouble with.

    Affirmations are written statements that are meant to keep you focused and motivated. Read them every day and your dreams will come true quicker than you could ever imagine. Each sentence can help you conquer your personal downfalls which will help keep you inspired on a daily basis if you read them consistently. They can be statements such as "I work out every day" or "I read every day" which I both recommend doing daily. Reading and exercising are two tasks that help get you to where you want to be because they strengthen the mind and body, but should only be a part of your daily routine if you enjoy partaking in these activities. Affirmations aren't for everyone but if you are new to them I recommend starting with ten or less. Here is a list of the ones that I have found to be most useful.

- I am happy
- I am content
- I can, I will, I choose to
- I am conscious of every breath I take
- I am complete
- I am whole
- I am eternal
- I live life to the fullest
- I live in the moment
- I do it now
- I work towards my dreams and goals every day
- I have everything my heart desires
- I am an infinite being
- I am healthy
- I am wealthy
- I respect all
- I love all of God's creations
- I am free
- I am peace
- I am love
- I love everyone and everything

## Relationships

Sometimes we must let go of unhealthy relationships to facilitate personal development for both parties. If you feel as if the people you hang out with are holding you back from evolving spiritually then it's okay to move on because you can always keep them in your heart and one day reconnect; if it's what you need then it's probably favorable for them as well. Everything that happens in life is necessary for the evolution of consciousness. It may be hard to see sometimes but it is all love.

A good relationship is one that is constantly giving and receiving acts of love, and is constantly striving towards growth and working to rid the body of toxins rather than accumulating them. Although you are responsible for your own inner-circumstance and decisions it can be difficult until you become fully present it is often easy to become like the people you hang out with. If you are in a close relationship with someone who is self-destructive, and you aware of this then love yourself and move on if you feel as if they are bringing you down. In order for a relationship to flourish space is so important because it allows both parties time for reflection on what they have learned thus far in their lives and allows for contemplation on what the next step needs to be.

Many of us don't realize it but some of the people we interact with including family, friend, or foe, drain us of energy on a daily basis. A truly uplifting relationship is one that contains an equal balance of giving and receiving, meaning that each person wholeheartedly listens as much as they speak. It is a special bond between beings in which one uses only supportive kind words after an idea is presented to the other. All you have to remember is to not let others take your love or time for granted. If you allow this to happen it does not help either person in the relationship. For a relationship to work well between two individuals it is necessary to stay present and focused on what is happening right now rather than what happened or what you think might happen. It is also very important to forgive one another for past mistakes. Not only this, but forgive yourself for past relationships that didn't work because recollecting these circumstances brings up feelings of guilt which will bring more of these experiences not allowing the relationship to grow. In general, most of the people we interact with, mainly our friends are very similar to the way we are. We can be influenced by the people we spend our time with in many ways. Therefore, if it is you desire to be blissfully happy or make more money, a great way is to befriend people who have what you want. Thinking the same way, eating the same food, and hanging out with the same individuals will get you the same results. As long as it causes no harm to yourself or those around you then I see nothing wrong with it, and in reality there is nothing right or wrong about anything we do because this is all just a constant learning experience. However, there is always a better way to think, eat, and socialize.

    A healthy relationship is one that is constantly giving and receiving acts of love. Although you are responsible for your own inner-circumstance and decisions, until you become fully present it is often easy to become like the people you hang out with. If you are in a close relationship with someone who is self-destructive, and you aware of this then love yourself and move on if you feel as if they are bringing you down. Trying to control others by relying on fear merely signifies a lack of desire to be filled with the Holy Spirit which governs the unlimited source of cosmic love.

## Making Changes

Although at the end of the day it really is our thoughts which cause us suffering, and it can easier to improve how we think by altering what we see and hear. For example, imagine taking a week or perhaps a month away from all music, television, in addition to all forms of media. If you have fearful thoughts that you don't enjoy then it's most likely that they stem from one of these sources. Before you can get what you want, you must find whatever your weakness is and take a break from it to learn how to see the beauty in everything. There is no time like the present to start making changes, but I have found that the best time is to start by going about your day differently as soon as you wake up. This is the time to begin new habits. Try going on a walk, meditating, or drinking a different kind of tea. My mornings always start with inverting, meditation, and drinking water.

We all use both hemispheres of our brain to help us go about our day. Without both sides it might be impossible to function by ourselves on a day to day basis. However, this is all hypothetical because if there is an injury to your brain it will adapt and rewire itself to survive. In general most of us typically use one side or the other which can be harmful or very beneficial to our well-being. The left hemisphere thinks in words and is said to be the rational or logical side. It is responsible for speech as well. The right is responsible for creativity, intuition, as well as envisioning. It has also been said to be responsible for our intuition and the emotions we feel. I have found that the best decisions of my life have been made based on how I felt rather than what my mind was telling me. The interesting fact is that each side controls the opposite side of the body and sees out of opposite eyes. So basically the best thing to do when your thoughts are giving you troubles is to look out of your right eye to see reality for the perfection that it really is. If your mind is daydreaming situations that do not bring you happiness or situations that you want to attract into your life, then try using your left hand or view life from the left eye. Ideally we want to focus with both eyes out of our peripherals, and use both hands as often as possible which stimulate the entire brain to maximize our full potential. The lyrics activate the left hemisphere and the tune stimulates the right. Listening to classical music, preferably piano, is fantastic for creative work because it synchronizes both hemispheres.

  The following activities are the ones I use most often to instantaneously feel better: walking, hugging, laughing, kissing, looking at far away objects, listening to my favorite music, singing, dancing, or spending time with loved ones. Studies have shown that standing and inverting helps prevent the ill effects of gravity on the human body. So if you are sitting a lot and you don't feel your best then simply stand up!

The last suggestion on making positive beneficial changes for your life is to let go of all the material items that you don't use or need. The ego is greedy, identities with material items, always desires more, and wants to hold on but it's so rewarding to stay strong from its clingy grasp. Give your stuff away, have a yard sale, donate your old clothes, and sell it on craigslist or Ebay. It is a gratifying freedom! Don't be cheap because it can be self-harming, however it is very wise to be thrifty!

Whatever it is you do with whomever, whenever you are doing it, accept, embrace, and love it with all your power which is all that is, even if you have yet to come to this realization at this point in infinite time. God loves all of us so much that we are given the choice in each moment to choose between the ultimate divine truth or mental programming of the ego. If we could all see more than what meets the eye we would all internalize that the eternity which we all choose is eternal.

## Purpose

One person views a fresh cut lawn as attractive. The next sees it as less oxygen-producing plants and more toxins in the air due to the byproducts from the lawn mower. Neither person is right or wrong because nothing is supposed to be a certain way; it really just is what it is. Everything in life is a matter of perception as well as perspective. Before one can truly find peace, rather realize it within, we must prior take accountability for our lives. This is where mentors and people to look up to come in handy pertaining to all areas of your life which include health, spirituality, and success. Everyone's definition of success is different, and your role models should have the things you want.

Without a purpose it can be hard to make permanent lasting inner and outer changes. One could be your kids, family, mankind, or God which is one that will lead you to a life of service and love. Unless they are spiritual, then your goals shouldn't define your purpose for living because material items typically don't give someone the true fulfillment we are all looking for. True presence reveals all that is needed in the perfect timing of existence.

The ego typically tries or wants to control everything in its path, but you have the power to let go of it. You have control over everything that you do as well as your reactions to everything that happens throughout your stay on this earth. Our ego labels events, material items as situations as good or bad pertaining to what it wants or does not want. There may appear to be two choices in life at all times, but actuality it is one path which is of light because that is only what truly exists in the divine infinite reality called the miracle of creation or God.

    The beliefs and more specifically the ego we hold on to are the reasons for not reaching full potential in this lifetime, but unless you were born enlightened and into an incredibly wealthy family then it is necessary to firmly understand it to succeed in today's day and age. What you believe should always be subject to change. The ego can be described as what you think, what you think you are, and the things which you have identified with the self. You are not your wife, your kids, your house, your car, or anything you think you are for that matter.

    A firm understanding of infinity allows each of us to breeze effortlessly through life. Everything and anything you can imagine is not only possible but it's happening. Some things in life are left unexplained because they can't be explained, but rather felt. The second you focus on love is the moment you start to attract amazing circumstances which bring exuberant feelings of gratitude into your existence. When you think how you want to it in turn helps to create your deepest desires from within if you so choose to believe in the power of yourself.

## Breathing

We can survive without food and water for quite some time but not oxygen. Most of us are hyperventilating, constantly taking short shallow breaths, yet we are not conscious of it. When you are feeling anxiety or stress this is usually why. Although most us think that toxins are eliminated out of the body via sweat, urine, or feces; science has found that seventy percent of toxins are actually released from the lungs! Breathing is the number one way to attract more energy from the universe right now, and it is free! It also changes your mood instantly! I breathe into my stomach by taking it in through my nose and releasing air through my mouth.

Right now I want you to put your hand on your stomach and breathe deep into your diaphragm. Breathe into your belly making it protrude. After your stomach is full of air, breathe through your lungs and imagine the air going up to your brain before finish the inhale. Through each inhale and exhale visualize the oxygen going through your nose, down to your stomach, up to your brain, and finally out through your mouth. Breathe, breathe, and breathe again. This is called diaphragmatic breathing and it is wonderful! Try it now repeatedly until you lose focus. When I am waiting for someone or something I have found that is the best time to practice meditation while breathing.

Aside from taking long walks, my favorite exercise is breathing. The best time to practice this is during times of meditation, while you are waiting for something or someone, or all day if you can manage it. Being aware of your breathing takes you from your thoughts and supplies your body with with more energy than food or drink can give you. Diaphragmatic breathing allows you to get more oxygen for less breath. The way to go about this is to breathe in through your nose into your stomach. If you take a big enough breath you can make your belly protrude. Next, breathe this air into your lungs, and then exhale. This method of breathing can make a huge difference in your health.

I strive to live my life by the biblical quote "eat to live and live to eat", especially knowing there are starving fellow human beings on the planet. However, I strongly want you to remember this next bit of advice. **Breathe to live and live to breathe!** Whenever you are feeling down or are being bothered by your thoughts this will cure you instantly. If there is one thing you take from this book and apply it to your habits I hope it is this.

# Chapter 2.) Enlightenment is the Way

To me, inner peace is more precious than gold, silver or anything on this planet. There may be many obstacles in your life that are holding you back from pure bliss on a moment to moment basis, but it is important to understand that everything is necessary for your own spiritual growth. In reality everything is one, happening of its own accord, facilitated by the grace of God. If we didn't think we knew an object was here, or over there then we would realize everything is everywhere and infinite. It's just the egoic mind that made up time and space which at times can cause us to feel alone or separated from our source which is God. However, you are never alone and you get to choose how you feel! This is helpful when attempting to attract something into your life because once you realize you are everything you believe you can manifest anything! The constant creation and evolution of life is a miracle that mustn't be taken for granted, actually it cannot be due to the effects of karma which can be transcended, endured here on this plane of existence, or fulfilled in another lifetime. With the population now over seven billion there are babies with old souls and eighty year olds that could still be very new to this experience.

In words, spiritual enlightenment could be described as a feeling within that you have the ability to access whenever you find it necessary to. It comes with the understanding that you control how you feel about your life, coupled with the realization from that you are so special because you are necessary for the universe to function. You were brought into this world to maintain the balance of energy that our universe functions on. For very few this feeling of oneness comes right away and others like myself it takes much practice. It took me many years before I truly understood that I have complete control over my life, thoughts, and my emotions. The motivation should be that you shall suffer no longer. As Jesus said, "The kingdom of heaven is within."

Whether we are aware of it most of us have dominate thought patterns and habits, which can make it hard for us to break self-destructive routines. Underneath all the chattering of the mind lies silence, once you let go of all thoughts, that will allow you to feel true bliss and peace of mind. If you continue to let your ego run your existence rather than feeling your way through each day then you will continue to get the same results in all areas of your life as well as feel the way you always do. There may appear to be two choices in life, but in actuality it is one path which is of light because that is only what truly exists in the divine infinite reality. God is the answer to all of

## 33 How to Be Happy and Live Life to the Fullest

your unanswered questions and enlightenment is the way to God!

## Acceptance

The first step to peace of mind is becoming aware of everything around you which includes your body, spirit, and surroundings. You are just as much the words you are reading as well as your toes feet and hands. Take five minutes and practice letting go of your thoughts while you occupy certain areas of the body. Search and surrender areas of stress that are typically located around the eyes, in the stomach, cheeks, and neck. If you are ever in a situation when the mind is racing this is the most effective exercise, aside from conscious breathing, that will bring you back to self-realization again. We are all equally everything that exists. Everything in reality is perfect the way it is or it would not be. The mind tends to ask "why?" when it is exposed to something that it does not want to, or cannot comprehend. God will always be the answer to all of your questions. Our body is guided by our soul, and our souls are guided by God. This is obvious when one realizes we have an innate ability for intuition, and the more in tune you are with God the smoother your life will go.

Science will continue to try to figure out the nature of reality but it's a never ending quest so just let them try to figure it out because God will always be the force that governs our being. Everything that has happened and is happening, whether you perceive it as good or bad, is necessary for the spiritual evolution of man. It is viewed as right or wrong due to the ego's judgment of what it wants or does not want. The more aware you become the more you realize that there is only one way which is the way of God through loving everything and everyone. Use discernment rather than judgment until you can step back and watch life take form. Life is more enjoyable as you participate in the everyday activities rather than let your ego run your life and make your decisions.

    We live in a society which the majority of people don't know what they want simply because all of us have not realized how powerful we really are yet. Believe it or not the life you live, as you read this sentence, came about as a collected result of every thought you have allowed and action you have created. The current situation of mankind is no single person or groups fault, but rather each individual's own resistance of what is best for the betterment of the human race. Before you can let go of the past and live in the present moment it is not only vital to accept your current life circumstance, but necessary to forgive and entirely accept yourself because thoughts of past situations you didn't agree with only cause anger within the self. If you have thoughts of sadness or think you are depressed then you are searching outside the self for approval, but you must go inside for acceptance and forgiveness. Stress and anxiety merely comes from our thoughts, usually causing physical pain. You don't have to feel bad! Underneath everything we think is the universal mind which is silent but powerful. What I mean is that the closer you get to God the more pleasant your thoughts become.

    Everything you see on a moment to moment basis can influence you towards bettering or worsening your life if you let it. The internet is a beautiful technology today that we can all learn from if we take advantage of it, specifically YouTube if you are listening to the right knowledge and wisdom. Use discernment along with your intuition as your guide. Years from now you will be incredibly appreciative if you allow yourself to live in moment at all times so as to not get misguided in anyway. Social media and the typical news coverage can create desires and fears within our own minds that are not truly ours, and is usually not of anything that is of real concern because it already happened. I firmly believe humanity is starting to wake up to realize that nothing is more precious than inner peace. Compassion for all that is living solves any problem that may arise in your life.

    The only reason you don't have everything you want is because you don't want it bad enough yet, or you don't truly want it. Before you can start taking action towards your dreams and goals it is necessary to take control of what you think. To let go of the ego is to let go of all pain. Being egoless allows you focus on everything you love. You can't be hurt or affected by anything that happens in your life because you are detached from everything but still present and very much aware. You can and will be very much at peace once you completely let go of comparing yourself to others and judgment.

    A lot of people go about their days with racing minds and negative thought patterns simply because they let their ego run their lives. There is so much doubt built up within the mind because as soon as we are first able to understand language we are constantly being told what to do and how to live our lives. So the mind tends to form thought patterns such as "I can't do that" or "I could never do that"; and these statements are in fact true if you choose to believe everything your mind tells you. Many people procrastinate simply because "do it later" pops up in their mind when an idea or task surfaces. You can change "do it later" to "do it now" which eliminates the problem of procrastination! Start now by listening to your thoughts for a few minutes….. It's okay to laugh at the absurdity of what you think sometimes! Step back and watch the ego try to wreak havoc on your physical, emotional, and spiritual well-being. Always accept and surrender to your thoughts rather than resisting. Let go of all that cause you suffering and surrender them to god.

Underneath all the thoughts that cause pain are the ones that bring joy and happiness. This is basically meditation and the more you do it the easier life becomes. The best time to practice is while waiting for someone or something throughout the day. If your body is not in good physical health then it sometimes can be more difficult to be at peace with your thoughts because all of your energy is focused towards removing toxicity. If you have beautiful, positive and uplifting thoughts then you attract a marvelous lifestyle.

    If you want to be happy, successful and healthy then you must learn moderation. Overdoing anything is the reason why unbalance and dissatisfaction will occur in your life. Making a lot of money is a good thing as long as it is made in a manner that betters mankind and is spent towards the good things in life which are supportive for the human race because there is karma for all actions. You are going to get what you think about most of the time. If you imagine the things you want to occur and firmly believe in them then they will happen, likewise with the things you don't truly wish for. So you must stay present at all times so that you do not attract anything in your life that you do not truly desire.

    The only reason we have thoughts that cause us to feel fear is because we have not faced, or accepted and let go of them to god yet. Anything you truly believe you can accomplish that you have yet to, will cause fear until it is achieved. The best way to get rid of that fear is to write the small steps down which help you achieve it. Lists are important before you can transcend the chatter of the ego which will allow you to live in the moment all the time. The egoic mind distracts, argues, and tries to bring other people down to make it feel superior. If you truly think you are better than another person then you have a lot to learn. There is no right or wrong way to do something. If you can look upon something as it is without judgment you are probably not judging yourself which is a beautiful miracle. If you having a hard time accepting and letting go of the thoughts that are holding you back then just know that it takes more practice. Focusing on different parts of the body such as the toes, stomach, brain, eyes, and hands will help you stop thinking if your thoughts are bothering you. Feel all throughout your body and let go of all the tensions. It is also possible to feel the entire body as one.

    All physical and emotional pain is in the mind. If you surrender and be totally present you will feel no pain whatsoever. Switch your attention to your breathing or focus within the body during these times. You are not that pain and you do not have to feel it. If you are feeling hurt from the loss of a relationship just know that the person is no longer in your life because you needed to realize that you need nothing outside of what you already have. Any relationship comes about to raise your level of consciousness. Don't become attached to anything in life because it's never permanent.

You can achieve, feel, and think or not think as you so wish. If you ever feel sorry for yourself then you have yet to come to the realization that you the creator of everything you see, feel, and believe. The first step is envisioning the life you want to live in the most vivid detail you so desire and write it down. Long-term goals should be written down or they must be instilled so deep within that the feeling of accomplishment is constantly being passed through the mind causing excitement. If you have these goals written down, truly believe you can accomplish them, and then your mind and body will take the necessary actions until your desires are met.

## Meditation

When most people think of meditation they think of monks sitting cross legged, but to me it is mindfulness. It's participating in, with full attention, whatever is in front of you at the time. Meditation brings you back to the moment and the key is to find what does this for you so that the mind does not race or imagine unwanted outcomes. It is a place of peace that we must all find on our quest of immortality. I have found taking walks, being in nature, as well as exercising to be some of the best ways to get of my mind and my body.

One way to get into a deep meditation is when you eat your food rather than watch tv or find some other sort of distraction during meals. I enjoy meditating before meals because it allows for the expression of gratitude. A lot of people hardly chew their food several times before they swallow it which doesn't allow them to breakdown all the carbohydrates, fats, proteins, vitamins and minerals which causes them to be overweight, malnourished, or results in skin issues. This used to be a very big problem of mine. Train your brain to think "chew your food" while you eat and eventually you will just do it without having to think about it. The more you chew your food the less you will eat and the more energy you will manifest. Eventually you can get so good at it that you will go into a state of meditation.

Meditation is something that you can practice everywhere all the time. You can be in a place of peace while still going about your day to day activities. You can allow God to run your life while you sit back and enjoy the show. You are infiniteness. You are God. If you make time to sit and be with your thoughts you will eventually have complete control over them which will help you in all areas of your life. If you start a sitting meditation practice don't set a time frame, as it is just a man-made illusion, but try to do it consistently on a daily basis to ensure ensuring beneficial results. Try listening to an "Om" chant, 528 Hz meditation, or other audio track without words to aid you in your practice.

    A great way to start taking control of your thoughts is to start a practice of meditation. I have found the best time to start is when you feel at peace. This will further the feelings that you enjoy the most. Try practicing it when you wake up or at night before dinner or around the time of going to bed. Don't resist your thoughts when they come in. This eventually allows all thoughts to subside. The more you practice meditating the easier it gets and the more you will want to do it. Practice meditation throughout the day whenever you can. Don't allow the mind to run your life or interfere on your happiness.

## Letting Go

For as long as human beings have been on the planet, it's mind-blowing that we've yet to get along. The world is such a beautiful place that was created for us to share and improve, not hoard and destroy. We are here to live in harmony with all that is. We make choices to the best of our ability until we let the Holy Spirit intervene entirely because only the divine know what is truly best for us. If your desire is to reach spiritual enlightenment then it is important to come to the realization that all attachments are what cause us pain. Life beyond death is only going to be as good as it is now. True presence reveals all that is needed in the perfect timing of existence. To acquire real, lasting inner peace one must let go of thoughts and feelings because they are connected.

Once you get to the source of the way you feel and think it is easy to understand that it is not being caused by anything else. Some people still believe that God is a man in the sky, but in reality God is just as much out there as in here because if not we would not be able to exist. God did not have to think to create the bodies we inhabit, the planet we reside on, or the infinite ever-expanding multi dimensional universe. If God was like most of us he or she would still be thinking and procrastinating about creating us and we would be without sentient bodies like all prophets, saints, sages, and enlightened beings that have walked the planet they found inner peace through surrendering their will to the Holy Spirit and by living through non attachment. Letting go of the illusion of time can allow more peace and presence to follow through your existence, and it is absolutely necessary for enlightenment. We make decisions and take steps towards what we feel is right, but at the end of the day God gives us what is best. For example, we take the initiative by going to college, applying for a job, going in the woods to hunt, foraging for food, making dinner, starting a family, or attempting to fly a kite, but the outcome is reflected by our inner relationship with God.

      The beautiful fact of the matter is that we all have the ability and choice to let go of what we think we are during this transitory experience, which are the thoughts that are holding us back from reaching our full potential. The truth of the matter is that we should because we are all much more special than we generally think we are! Once complete we will all let go of judging ourselves and others! Our physical bodies house a spirit that is craving freedom but we must learn to control what we think and do, so we do not hurt others or the planet. Once we all decide to live in the moment, find ourselves, and become conscious beings then there will be no more arguing, fighting, or killing. Remember, to let go of the ego we must first regularly monitor and accept our thoughts as much as possible, and strive to embrace and understand why we have these thoughts that we do not enjoy. We must all accept that problems that arise stem from past actions.

## Silence

    I've grown accustom to the silence because within the senseless chatter is the truth, and beyond this lies an inner peace which is the only real security in this lifetime. What I mean is that if you listen to your thoughts enough they guide you towards eternal bliss. God wants you to be happy, wants you to feel joy all the time, but how can you if you do not allow the divine infinite energy to fill your body. You know you are in the presence of the Holy Spirit when your mind is silent. Until one accepts everything in their life then they will continue to let the ego run their life, which I have found to be quite exhausting. Surround yourself with brilliant conscious entities who are devoted to living a healing holistic life. Friends who have flexible long-term goals they are determined to accomplish while living a balanced existence on this wonderful planet we all call home. Leading others down the right path is as simple as cherishing the considerate ways of naturalness. Be fair, accepting, generous, as well as forgiving because it allows you to be free and detached from your ego. Allow yourself to be sober to allow vivid clarity at all times. Open your mind up to the possibility that everything is possible because it truly is.

    If you choose to have a beautiful abundant lifestyle then it is not only wise but necessary to start believing in everything you do. Whether you are aware of it or not there is an intention of fear or love behind every action you commit, meaning that everything you do determines humanities outcome. You are responsible for everything you do which is why it is wise to be ethical in your decision making processes. Be generous, kind, and polite towards everyone because having compassion for all that is living is the most joyous privileged life. Learn to love everything and everyone. Sharing your love on a global level is free the moment you realize how powerful you are.

      If you really want something to happen in this world and it aligns with the purpose god has for you then it will happen with enough prayer. Feel as if it already happened and visualize it, don't just ask for it. The only way to feel secure in this lifetime is to acquire inner peace by surrendering to, and maintaining presence while being. We are all creators created by the creation. Everything is possible that you can imagine because it's happening right now. We contribute to the infinite expansion of consciousness! The world is a beautiful place for all of mankind to enjoy! Love is the solution!

# Chapter 3.) Manifesting Your Desires

Have you ever wondered if there was an easier way to get what you want? Well there is and it is a universal law that is commonly called the law of attraction (even though it is often not taught correctly), and it goes hand in hand with spiritual enlightenment. Diligence is key when it comes to making more money, or attracting anything you want in life. When it comes to the things you desire never put limits on yourself because you have unlimited power. Before one can manifest their desires it is necessary to understand that we live on a planet with unlimited abundance. However, the mindset must be there to attract it. There can be enough food to feed the entire planet sevenfold if we change our diet which I'll talk about in the last chapter, and there is enough money, assets, and wealth in circulation right now for every single person to be a millionaire. Let me just say that again. **We all can be millionaires!** It's just up to you to attract it which starts by ceasing to have thoughts of the lack of what you want. You have to love money to make money. Many people can't hold on to money because of their attitude towards it from past experiences. Change your thoughts and you change your life.

The brain is a transmitter and receiver of energy or in another term frequency, and when you emit a thought it comes back in a similar if not identical form. Manifestation occurs consciously and subconsciously. Believe it or not thoughts are things. Words that have been said to me have hurt more than most of the physical pain I have endured at times in my life. If you put out a frequency, it is picked up by other matter whether it be other humans or objects. This is crucial to grasp because what you think about you get, most of the time, whether you perceive it as good or bad.

First things first, anything you want will only come into existence if you truly believe in it, and a great way to do this is to feel as if you already have it. Daydreaming and visualization are superb tools for manifesting if they are used in a manner that supports what you are trying to accomplish. I am a firm believer that anyone can get whatever they want as long as it aligns with God's purpose for them. Another reason you might not get what you want is because it won't help you on your spiritual path if that's where you're headed. What I mean is that if what you want is selfless, loving, and beneficial for all of mankind or at least the people around you then you are most likely going to get it and usually quicker than you might assume. It all comes down to the intentions we have because at the end of the day we do not manifest what we want, we manifest what we are, act, think, and feel.

First of all, you must always follow your own intuition and secondly only take advice from the people who you feel are sincere and have what you want. Mentors in all areas of your life regarding finances, health, and spiritual will help you get where you want to go. This is very important so that you are not misguided in any way by people who are misinformed. When you use the law of attraction properly, you get anything and everything your heart desires as long as you truly believe in what you want. You choose your destiny. You have complete control. The fastest way to change or better your life is to alter or improve the way you think. It takes practice or sometimes a sudden desire of no longer wanting to suffer in order to gain complete control over your thoughts, but with this comes inner peace. Remember we are not our thoughts but the thoughts we have determine what happens in our life because what you think about regularly, you get most of the time. This is the first basic concept of the law of attraction. It is the law that you can use to get whatever you want and I will go into more detail now. Before I begin you must understand that the moment you stop learning, is the instance your life stops getting better. The more willing you are to learn from the people who have what you want along with the more accepting you are of change, the better your life will be.

Everything on the planet has been proven to be made of the same atoms, just different configurations, or in other terms the same exact type of material, just different amounts of space between substances. The mesmerizing fact is that virtually every atom is virtually all space! The more scientists try to see what substances are made of the more they see vast space. This is important to understand because it is proof that any being can attract anything and everything they desire if enough focus is applied towards the outcome. I also believe enlightenment is connected to the realization when you understand we all have the choice and power to do or think whatever we please.

I'm going to say it again, because it is very important to understand, humans are extraordinary in my eyes because our brains are transmitters and receivers of energy! It is obvious when one looks around in their home or city and sees that everything we are nearly surrounded by was once a thought in a human being's mind. Every thought you have has been proven to affect physical matter which is very obvious when you realize that you did not create certain thoughts that pass through your mind. This means that frequencies transmitted by humans pass through all matter. The intensity is set forth in your mind and travels as far as the desire you put forth in it. When you are excited, this is a high energy thought meaning it can affect physical matter on the other side of our planet. Frequencies actually pass through all matter which makes sense when you consider that science has proven everything is virtually space the more they try to isolate molecules, which proves we should just work with we nature provides for us. But this means that if we concentrate with enough energy on we want, or actually whatever we regularly think about, then eventually it will be present in our life. This is the reason why you must practice visualization of whatever you desire because you will actually bring it forth into your life faster if you focus strong enough! The greater the concentration, the quicker whatever we are thinking about will manifest into our lives, good or bad. If we are not at peace with our thoughts then we are not enjoying our time on this planet, and we are not transmitting frequencies of the things we desire. After all, we collectively receive nearly everything we think about on a daily basis. For example, if you are feeling anxious, then situations or people that make you feel anxious will occur in your life. If you want a certain car then you must think about it and visualize yourself in it until it appears into your life. Before you can start to transmit powerful frequencies your body must first feel good all the time, and you must clearly define what you want so that you know what need to be thinking about.

    We all know what we need to do deep down. Stress is a motivator and a signal from our body to make us move. It's up to you where to guide it. It's only detrimental to our health when we let it accumulate by procrastinating. The key is to focus on one thing at a time to maximize productivity and minimize stress.

## Intentions

Intentions are one of the most important aspects of attracting more abundance into your life. Life is a constant process of giving and receiving. It may stray out of balance for a short period of time but it always go back into equilibrium. If you want to get more you have to give more. Someone might say, "well how do I get more money if I don't have to any to give." Life is far more deeper than what our eyes can depict. Say you give a random stranger a compliment. That positive energy radiates to that person which they in turn share on to the next person. This energy eventually comes back to us. In fact all energy we put out into the universe comes back to us at some point or another. Give love and you will in turn receive whatever you want. You get what you give and we all get what we deserve. The power of prayer is so profound and any large feat is easily accomplishable with it, but keep in mind the whole human race when you pray and that will help all of us get what we're looking for. When I pray I pray for everyone because I feel it is the right thing to do.

There is karma for everything we do until we reach a certain level of awareness in which we are in a continuous state of peace, love, and gratification. If we have selfish intentions then most likely our desires will not be fulfilled and if they are the manifestation will only short term feelings of pride. Being proud of our accomplishments can be better than most emotions that some of us feel on a daily basis, but it does not even compare to feelings of gratitude, love, and joy. Loving heartfelt intentions that are beneficial to the entire human race are the ones that manifest the fastest. Also, the more powerful the intention the quicker the intention manifests into your reality. I have used the following technique numerous times to attract desires into my life instantaneously. First you must clearly envision what you want in your mind until you get a vivid visualization. Then focus this energy to your heart and feel the emotion that you would have once this desires comes into your life. Next, you must let go of all attachments so that it can manifest into your reality. Many people don't fully surrender their desires to God, which is why they never happen. Until you wholeheartedly let go of all you wants, they will not occur in your life. The more practice at this technique the better you will get at it. Apply it to every aspect of your life. Let go of useless thoughts and emotions with it and set the intention for them not to come back. It is a flawless wondrous miracle-working technique that could be described as prayer, and never forget that it first starts in the belief of the mind. You are capable of everything you can imagine, but remember that there is always karma for all actions and thoughts.

Everything in your life, whether you like it or not, has been created by you. To alter your thoughts to transmit beneficial frequencies you must first acquire complete control over your thoughts. A good way is to start is by recollecting, or physically writing down everything you are thankful for in the morning and before going to sleep at night. I love to do this in the sun in the morning and at night. The sun and the earth are the two things I am most grateful for because they provide us with life. Practicing this daily attracts a grateful attitude which in turn will bring about people, situations, and things that you bring you feelings of gratitude.

Consistent productivity is where a lot of people struggle and this is because the passion isn't there. There are three concepts to productivity that must be mastered to get what you want. They are time intervals, reward systems, and energy cycles. Until trained well the human mind can only stay focused for so long. Set the time you want to work for and stick with it then take a short break and do it again. Try working in intervals of around an hour, but it's up to you to find your happy medium. Be careful what you eat and when you try to work. Don't force yourself to work, such as right after waking up from, when it doesn't feel right. Don't expect to be productive after eating a large meal, especially of fat. Try eating a few pieces of fruit and always give yourself some time for digestion before working.

## Desires

Don't just expect miracles, make them happen! Our goals usually stem from the things we want, which is understandable, but step back to see why you want whatever it is you do. Before I get into goal setting, I want to talk about the desires you have. A lot of the wishes we have stem from the people we study, follow, spend out time with, and look up to. Realize that the reason have them because you're attracted to what they have, what they represent, and the energy of these people. Their consciousness. You have the ability to reach that level of power and feel how you want. Most of us have many desires but until the belief of the achievement is completely instilled within the mind or written down then it is most likely that they won't be achieved. To achieve your goals the strong belief in them must be entirely present. Any doubt in the mind inhibits your body from taking action. Rather than just writing down all the things you want, which I do recommend doing, it helps if you first become at peace with your thoughts while getting to know your authentic self.

Motivation and ambition either come from fear or love; it's up to you to choose. The more you are crossing off accomplishments off your list the faster your dreams are going to come true. Everyone has their own method to be productive. One is to find ways to reward yourself after completion of the tasks with things such as nourishing food, reading, or social media (specifically YouTube because it is a great tool for learning), and the other is to just do it out of sheer desire of will and love. Begin with a yellow tablet or notebook for your list, and if you want to live a life of gratitude then before you start your day or go to sleep at night, focus on everything you are grateful for. I am always grateful for breathing. I love being able to breathe. Also, before or after your gratitude session each night, clearly define what tasks you are going to accomplish the day beforehand.

If you want to feel free from the anxieties brought on my money, brainstorm ways to make money so you can eventually not have to work for an employer because you'll end up being a slave to the system if you don't start to get out now. The system is designed to keep you in debt and you'll never be free or make any large amounts money working a nine to five job because the guy at the top is making it all.

I recommend starting by brainstorming ideas for a business or another source of income. The internet is a great place to start making extra money when you're trying to make money on your own. You can write e-books, buy and sell items on eBay, craigslist, or make money doing YouTube videos, but ideally you want to start some sort of business and find a way to generate passive income. Two areas that I believe will be of interest to people in the coming years are health and technology. I value freedom over finances which is why I started growing my own organic produce. To save money you can raise your own food and/or grow it, which allows you to rely on society less bringing more feelings of freedom. Living off the land brings me the most rewarding feelings of joy that I have ever known.

## Goals

Aside from setting your purpose, a wonderful way to attract more gratitude into your life is to have written goals. Look to create ones that have meaning along with value for all of society because these are the goals that manifest in record time. There are many creative ways that you can help yourselves and others in the same process. Right now I want you to get a pen, preferably blue, and a notebook. The first list I want you to write out will be what you want to accomplish in life. Most of mine are in the form of short sentences and you can have as many as you desire. These goals can be specific but I advise them to be general, with no time limits because the universe provides you with what you need at the exact time you need it. These statements should make you excited when you read them. If they do not then most likely it isn't what you truly want. The most important factor is that they must be written as if you already have them so that no doubt comes into your mind when you read them, and you can include them in your affirmations. If a particular goal involves money, and you don't feel good when reading it, then most likely the amount is too high at this point in time. A good way to write a goal involving money is, "I have more money coming in then I know what to do with." Like I said when writing out your desires it is crucial that they must be written as if you already have them. For example, if you want a car or say a ford truck then you should write it out as "I have" instead of "I will have" so that when you visualize your vehicle of choice it will bring no thoughts of doubt. Also, I recommend that your goals are not specific because the universe will provide you with what is best for you at the right timing, likewise you may change your mind on what you want as I have at times. I often rewrite mine, because they change as I become less materialistic and more at peace. I recommend to start with around fifteen or less but like I said you should have as few or as many as you feel fit. However, here are two that I highly recommend, the first of which is "I have inner peace" and the second is "I feel good all the time." In my opinion, you will never go wrong if you strive for these two.

    Once you have your written long term goals read them as often as possible and put them in a safe place where you can see them. Never get discouraged or they won't come into existence. Once you have the long term goals in place, your subconscious brain will work at finding the path to get there which I call short term goals because the faster you accomplish what you know you need to do the end result will manifest into existence. Put time limits on short term goals to maximize productivity but not long term. When it comes to goals always ask yourself what not how to avoid doubt and fear. The universe always provides exactly what you need at exactly the right time. You should feel ecstatic when you read your goals, and if not then it's probably because the desire is not fully there. Even if your long term goals seem way out of reach, with enough focus on what you want rather than how you will get it, the manifestation of these goals come into your reality in correlation to how quickly you surrender the energy to God as well as the intensity of the belief you have in the desire of this existence of form in your reality. We are all capable of manifesting anything and everything our heart desires.

    For many years now I've had a list of tasks that I can be working on in any given moment of the day. The key here is to feel good when you are doing any sort of work, whether it be creative or not. This in turns makes you not only want to do more but actually reinforces the habit so work eventually becomes an actual enjoyment. This is an incredibly effective way to get things done. The wonderful beauty of it all is that they never go anywhere so you don't have to work at crossing off the tasks on your list every day. I've found it handy to keep paper along with a writing utensil somewhere in the vicinity at all times or a cell phone works just as well, but it's important to be open for constant ideas. Once you firmly set the intentions of your long term goals the steps you need to get there will come about very often and spontaneously.

With enough focus and discipline all the small achievements lead to the accomplishment of your larger desires. Take one step at a time, but realize that every decision you make as well as every thought you allow into the existence of your experience affects the ultimate outcome of your reality. As Aristotle said, "We are what we repeatedly do. Excellence, then, is not an act, but a habit."

Writing out lists has tremendously helped me become an organized person! Whether they pertain to daily routine, reminders, gratitude, groceries, or material items I strongly recommend everyone have some sort of writing involved in their everyday lives. It allows you to express creative energy that builds up in addition to providing natural stimulation by teaching your brain to transmit frequencies. If you want to feel better every day then the best ways to relieve stress is by writing. If there are tasks we truly want to do, or material items we have desires for then they will remain as trapped energy in our brains until fulfilled. The best way to relieve this stress is by writing whatever we want down. Good thoughts and ideas often slip our minds because we do not have a pencil and paper nearby. Writing what you want or love down is also important because some tasks take more time to accomplish than others and some things may slip our mind.

Before I start and end every day I practice

gratitude for my breathing and I remember do this this because I have a yellow tablet that contains my daily activities in a list. On top it says, Breathe! Then the list is as followed:
- Gratitude
- Invert
- Meditation
- Stretch/Yoga/Exercise
- 12-4
- Cold Showers
- Work
- Learn/Love
- Gratitude

The 12-4 symbolizes time to get in the sun, and reminds me to do so. Although I don't always exercise I do start my day off with a handstand against my wall followed by meditation because they make me feel my best and keep me focused throughout the day.

  You can immensely improve your time on this planet by bettering your organizational skills. If your desire is to make a lot of money then a good way is to read and write often. All financially wealthy people are avid readers. Participating in these forms of mental stimulation allows you to create new neuro pathways because every time you learn something your brain creates a new connection for signals to travel, thus allowing your brain to let go of harmful thinking through old neuro pathways. However, the bottom line is that if you don't feel good you will not get what you want in life and you will not be able to accomplish your goals.

## Sexual Energy

Lastly, I want to talk about sexual energy and I can't emphasize the importance of this enough when it comes to well-being. Master your sexual energy! I'm so grateful for sex because after all we wouldn't be here without it! However, when trying to manifest thing into your life it can be a block for many reasons. Releasing this energy too much causes you to eat more to rebuild these hormones, fluids, and brings the desire to release it more because of all the feel-good neurotransmitters that are released. It is better to use it as a reward than a habit or ritual. We were born to create regardless whether it be children, success, or things we don't want.

All of us are receivers and transmitters of unseen energy. Say you give someone a compliment; this in turn sends them some positive energy that they in turn keep sharing to others throughout the day. This is relevant to sexual energy in that if you focus on it you can shift this energy to other areas of your life that need attention. Try going months without exerting this life force, this includes masturbation, and I guarantee you will accomplish the things you have been putting off. Focus on true unconditional love which is the love of all of God's creations. Your energy levels and attention span will be higher than they've ever been. A clear picture and a burning desire of what you want must be instilled within your mind so that everyday distractions do not get in the way of its accomplishment. We are meant to create even if it doesn't happen every time we have sex, and it takes a lot of energy to create another living being. If we take our focus off the usual intentional failed attempts at creation we can redirect our energy towards the things we want, and actually manifest them as quick as you imagine them.

    If you want to be able to have the focus you need make all of your dreams come true, then I cannot stress how important it is to master your sexual energy. We all love sex and if you're putting it off then there is nothing wrong with that either. Sex is one of the best ways to relieve stress and get out of your head but it is also one of the most energy depleting.

    If you really have a strong burning desire to accomplish something but can't seem to focus on the task then you might need to learn how to master your sexual energy. The body can be more concerned about keeping our genetics going and sometimes we let our desires get the best of us. Releasing these energies too frequently can be quite exhausting. You can be sexually fulfilled whenever you decide it within the mind. You have the power to remain in a state of bliss higher than any feelings that anything, outside of yourself, can bring.

## Chapter 4.) Feel Good All the Time

    No human being should have to suffer in any way at all. Although some days challenge our emotions and outlook on life, I believe it is possible for all of us to always feel content if we accept and surrender to each moment. If you want to master your life it is not only important, but rather necessary to take complete control over your own physical health which I explain you how to do so in this chapter. Any ailment you have doesn't have to be felt because you are that powerful, but it also can be cured as quickly as you imagine and believe. Before you can get what you want it is important to first feel good physically, mentally, emotionally, and spiritually. If your body is not running as optimally as you would like there are numerous ways to achieve this so that you can accomplish all your dreams with ease. If you are not physically feeling as good as you think you should, or not taking as much action as you want to be, then chances are your body isn't as nourished as it can be or it is too toxic. Science has proven that disease roots from two sources which are toxicity and malnutrition.

    Before anything, the first step is to believe in yourself as well as be confident that you can achieve and deserve to have radiant health. You must believe that you can have unlimited energy, because after all you come from it and are made of it. Although the oldest woman on the planet attributes her longevity to her consumption of chocolate, which is considerably valid due to the fact that raw cacao (the plant source from which chocolate is made of) has more antioxidants than any other food; becoming aware of your breathing is probably the next best concept to master due to the fact that it takes your mind away from taxing thoughts which drain you of energy as well as supplies your cells with oxygen which is the most abundant mineral on earth. As odd as this may sound studies have shown that the fewer calories you consume the longer you live. The oldest living recorded living human being a man from China who was two hundred and fifty six! He was an herbalist and lived mainly on teas.

    If you want to heal your body from the inside out from anything that you are suffering with whether it be physical, emotional, or spiritual, including all the toxins that we have been accumulating from birth, then I am here to help you accomplish your wishes. As simple as it may sound you have the power to heal your mind, body, and spirit if you just believe! The roots of all physical disease clearly come the thoughts you think, toxicity, and nutrient deficiencies. Three issues that can be alleviated very easily once the proper awareness is gained.

    If you want to lose weight for good or gain

weight then I can teach you how to do so if you are truly willing to make the necessary adjustments from within. Depending on how bad you truly want these changes correlates directly to how fast you will see real results. So basically what I mean is that you must believe in yourself as well as envision what you want to be, and practice feeling how you want to feel. It is important to start by consistently but slowly implementing the modifications discussed so they become habits, and every day you will feel better and have more and more energy as time goes on. Participating in simply half of these lifestyle techniques will add many years to your life along with those around you. I'm writing this because I care about you, and everyone else on this planet.

With today's knowledge and understanding I believe we should all be living well past ninety years of age or more, especially considering the oldest living woman is now a hundred and twenty seven years old! If your desire is to feel and look your best then the willingness to make changes in your everyday routines must be present first. You are the creator of your reality. If you're not happy with your life it's because you are letting your mind tell you that you are not happy. Your thoughts control your actions which in turn create the way you look and feel. If you want to alter your lifestyle for your benefit or accomplish something new it can only be done if you learn to let go of doubtful thoughts. You can have anything and everything your heart desires!

A fast path to optimum wellness is to identify all the matters that are holding you back and write them down, and then come up with a list of solutions that will cure you from these ailments. Don't focus on the list that you have trouble with because if you do you will only get more of that, simply use it to come up with a list of solution. Keep the list of the tasks that you want more of. For example, if you watch too much TV then maybe you might want to walk more. Another issue could be your weight. If you want to lose weight it might not be that you eat too much, but not enough of the right types of food. The right balance of whole foods will get you where you want to be. Write down whatever it is you want to achieve or become. Don't let doubt come into your life. Be all that you want to be and always believe in yourself.

Although the current methods of the conventional food supply has supplied us with an abundance of food, it also has supplied us with many toxins that are not natural to our bodies. The key to physically feeling your best in every given moment is to eliminate all toxins from your life and increase the amount of whole foods. Any processed food is toxic to the human body. The only reason many of us eat so much is because the food we eat is greatly lacking in minerals, enzyme, and vitamins which causes us to eat large amounts while can be very harmful to the human body, especially if they are processed foods. It also takes a lot of our energy to digest cooked foods which is why most of us have no energy. It is so simple to live a holistic lifestyle once you know how! This means of living relies on the whole experience as well as nature rather than synthetics made by people which to me has been proven to be more simple and peaceful. Not only will it increase longevity of you, but also the planet! When you reconnect with everything the earth provides for us you have the ability and power to feel good all the time! With today's knowledge and understanding I believe we should all be living well past ninety years of age or more, especially considering the oldest living woman from Mexico is now a hundred and twenty-seven!

## Water

The average person's tap water contains nearly 300 different chemicals, many of which are pharmaceuticals which have leached into the ground. A lot of people would agree that they need to drink more water on a daily basis. There really is no particular way to do anything in life, but there is always room for improvement. I weigh about a hundred and fifty pounds and I generally drink at least a gallon of water a day, sometimes more sometimes less, which is a hundred and twenty eight ounces or sixteen cups. Some experts recommend drinking an ounce per pound of bodyweight per day and some recommend half this amount, but it's up to you to find what works best for you. Although one person's truths are not another I can almost guarantee that if you slowly incorporate more into your diet you will continually have more energy day after day as well as better digestion and elimination.

So many individuals are dehydrated, and don't know what it feels like to be hydrated because they never have been. The lack of water causes the inside of their bodies to be sticky because of the deficiency of water in the cells. Slowly work your way up to drinking more until you find what works best for you, but don't force anything. Organic coconut water is a great way to speed up the process because they are high in electrolytes which allow your cells to take in the water. If you have access to young green coconuts this can be a great way to take your health and hydration to a new level.

Clean water is what your body craves. I think that many people don't drink enough water because they don't have access to clean water and aren't even aware of it. Chemically treated tap water from your city is some of the most toxic water on the planet and although any filter is better than no filter I have found the best to be a reverse osmosis system, steam distiller, gravity filter, or you can gather your water from a reliable spring which can be found at findaspring.com. I don't mean spring water from bottles because the plastic leaches out hormone-disrupting chemicals, such as BPA others, which the water picks up. True spring water is so valuable because it comes from very deep depths of around two thousand feet, making it very clean from toxins, mineralized, and bioavailable for our cells because it is compressed and dense. Most man-made wells get water from around a hundred and fifty feet deep. I prefer spring water but if I don't have access to it I opt for the best water I can find. Drink only when you are thirsty. Do what makes you feel best. You may look back one day and realize that simply drinking more water was one of the best decisions you've ever made as I have. Two very valuable concepts to keep in mind about water are some is better than none because we are practically made of it entirely, and any filter is better than no filter.

    There are several ways that you can jumpstart the hydration process which I have found to be incredibly effective in regards to my physical well-being. The first is to always drink water before you eat meals, and especially when you wake up. I drink at least sixteen ounces upon rising or eating, generally more. Without the proper amount of potassium and sodium in your body your body's cells won't be able to intake the extra water you are putting in your system. All raw foods are high in potassium, the most common one probably being bananas. Most people get plenty of salt in their diet but it is important to find your balance of potassium and sodium for proper hydration.

    Squeezing a half of or a whole lemon into a cup of water when you rise first thing in the morning is another valuable method for achieving optimal wellness and hydration. Lemon water triggers the liver to secrete bile which helps break down food, resulting in fabulous digestion. Studies have shown that if you use warm water it is more effective. I store all my water on the counter rather than the fridge because it takes unnecessary energy to heat cold water up to your body's temperature, but some health experts recommend drinking cold water to speed up your metabolism. If you can't drink lemon water because it is too bitter then I suggest drinking it with stevia powder or liquid extract. It's an herb that has no negative effects on the human body, making it the safest sweetener known to man. If you desire sugar then opt for organic due to the fact that conventional is made from genetically modified beets, making them very toxic to the human body. Coconut sugar or lo han guo are other safer alternatives as well.

So like I said the first step to take towards radiant well-being is to start with is hydration. You can drink water all day but you won't hydrate your cells if you don't consume enough potassium from raw foods, along with sodium from sea salt. Make sure to drink plenty of filtered water. If you choose to drink spring water then I recommend buying a tds meter to check for purity and pH.

We have been known to live without food for quite some time but water is a different story. It has been found that the exact percentage of water on the planet is exactly the same amount that is in our bodies. It flushes toxins through your system that have built up and cures your dehydration from the night allowing you to feel much better. Water can be purified in a countless number of ways using filters. Fluoride and chlorine are two very harmful chemicals they use to treat drinking water in some cities. Nearly all countries have banned fluoride from their drinking water but the United States. The chemical is also used when making conventional pesticides, vaccines, and has been found in nearly all processed food on the shelves because of the fluoridated water that is used to process it. More on this subject can be found at fluoridealert.org and it is definitely a website to check out. I highly recommend that you throw out your fluoride toothpaste and replace it with coconut oil, and/or plain (aluminum-free) baking soda. It is an extremely toxic substance that is derived from fluorosilicic acid which comes from trapped air pollution control devices used in the phosphate fertilizer industry. Both Hitler and Stalin used fluoride to sedate people and make them infertile so it's not something that has ever been used of good intentions regardless of what your dentist tells you. Healthy teeth start from the inside out not the other way around.

    Like I said only more expensive filters can remove fluoride, such as a reverse osmosis system or a water distiller. The only problem with filtering water is that it strips it of all the minerals, although less minerals is better than putting toxins into your body. Some health experts claim that when you use a water filter it causes the water to be unstructured and supposedly a water ionizer or a water alkalizer can restructure it but they are not cheap. There are many free ways to restructure your water. One is to cool it in the refrigerator and spin it in a glass jar so that it forms a vortex. As far as minerals go you can add a half a teaspoon of pink Himalayan salt to each gallon you make. Scientific studies have found that if you that if you tell your water you love it, with true intention, or write love on a piece of paper and tape it to your water container it restructures itself. This goes to show how powerful we really are. I find this to be of useful information, and believe it wise to pray over and bless anything that I put into my body whether it be food or drink.

    I have a reverse osmosis system and I gather spring water as I can. Any filter is better than no filter but I strongly believe it can be very beneficial to drink spring water as long as it is clean due to its high mineral content, and compressed (due to gravity) hexagonal configuration of water molecules that makes it more bioavailable to our cells. Water from springs comes from depths of two thousand feet or more, so if the earth can't provide us with natural, clean mineralized water I don't know what can. The water from fresh fruit and vegetable juices also provides our cells with dense water that hydrates them thoroughly. Living a holistic lifestyle is not only healthy for you, but greatly improves the quality of our planet by reducing the need for all the unnecessary manmade substances. I recommend that you drink at least sixteen ounces or more of water before every meal as well as before you consume any food every morning. If you are overweight and do not drink a lot of water start out slow by drinking one hundred and twenty eight ounces which is approximately a gallon per day. You will be amazed as the pounds disappear!

    The last, but most effective, cellular hydration technique I want to share with you is juicing. Smoothies are great, and I'll admit that I do consume a lot of the water I drink in smoothies, but juices are a whole level of health. Consuming fresh homemade fruit and vegetable juices provides your body with truly bioavailable nutrition due to the fact that there is no fiber to break down. If you've never had a juice then I suggest starting with carrots and celery which are high in potassium and sodium. Greens vegetables are some of the most nutrient dense foods to juice, and they mix well with apples to take away the bitterness. Juicing is so beneficial for the body because it is full of micronutrients. Many people are getting plenty of macronutrients which include carbohydrates, fats, and proteins. Micronutrients are all the minerals that your body needs to run optimally. There are around ninety different minerals that the human body needs and about a hundred and eight that have been identified, many of which in incredibly small amounts. However, the conventional food supply only puts three different minerals back into the soil. This causes the body to become unbalanced. If you don't have a juicer you can invest in a cheap one for less than thirty dollars. I got my first two that were used for less than five dollars apiece. Best investments of my life!

## Food

The next step is changing your diet to one that is free from man-made toxins so that your body can run more efficiently. I change my diet every day! I forage for as much wild food as I possibly can because it is free and science has proven that it contain a higher nutritional content of vitamins and minerals than store bought food. There are around 250,000 to 300,000 known edible species of plants around the planet. I feel that if more people knew how much free food there was they would be in nature more in search of it because let's face it, everyone loves free food!

For some reason I've noticed that people struggle most when it comes to eating healthy. I suppose we could attribute it to the abundance of genetically engineered, fast, and processed food in grocery stores. The best way to overcome this is to simply throw out all the food that you know is harmful in your house and replace it with foods made of love. The first step is become aware as to what is optimal for the human body. However, at the end of the day something is only going to harm you if you think it is, but when you make a conscious decision to eat healthy organic food it will be abundantly inexpensive for everyone. This will in turn make the world a better place for all of us. As Hippocrates said, "Let food be thy medicine and medicine be thy food."

Don't let anyone tell you there is a right

amount of fat, carbohydrates, or proteins you should to be eating. We all have different bodies with different needs. If there is something you want to change or improve about your body, know that it is possible through the help of mind and food. If your body is overweight it's probably an iodine deficiency due to the fact that this is your thyroid gland's main fuel source. Your gland uses this mineral to control your metabolism.

    Science is quickly proving that a plant-based diet is more optimal for the human body. The two most common myths people believe are that you need meat for protein and milk for calcium. A vegan strongman named Patrik Baboumian has been breaking world records, one of which where he carried 550 kilograms (1212.54 pounds) for 10 meters (32.81 feet), and milk actually leaches milk from your bones in order to digest but if you're going to drink it opt for raw from your local farmer. Although I am not against eating meat, eggs, or milk I completely aware of the ill effects of it the body. I choose to eat an all raw vegan diet because I've done the research, and it can be the healthiest lifestyle if done properly. There are also many raw vegan bodybuilders which demystify the average person's beliefs on the subject. I find it most optimal for my body. If you desire radiant health then I recommend learning everything you need to know about it before transitioning to this diet. I've read that if humans all became herbivores there would be enough food to feed the entire planet sevenfold, curing starvation and ending world hunger.

In order for your body to break down food to convert it into energy it must produce digestive enzymes. It takes eighty percent of the bodies energy do this, and the studies show that your body can only produce so many digestive enzymes within one lifespan. Raw plant foods contain digestive enzymes. The fresher they are the more enzymes they contain. If you want quick long lasting energy that will give you energy all day, without the crash, then reach for the fruit and/or raw foods. If you want to lose weight, no matter how much you eat, and have more energy than you've ever had then try transitioning to a raw plant-based diet. It is also very possible to gain weight on a raw vegan diet if you increase your fat and protein intake with intense training and/or weight lifting. They have done studies on the longest-lived people and what they like to eat. The top five longevity foods as a collective include all vegetarian sources as followed: chocolate, cinnamon, red onions, olive oil, and honey. Whatever you eat, opt for organic or homegrown and preferably raw.

Organic foods are important for a number of reasons. They cannot be irradiated or produced with toxic chemicals such as pesticides, herbicides, fungicides, or larvicides. They also cannot be grown from genetically modified seeds or irradiated. Irradiation is a food preservation process that destroys all the healthy bacteria, and it also has been proven to destroy vital nutrients. It is illegal to irradiate organic food which is another one of its perks. Local and homegrown organic fresh fruits and vegetables are the safest as well as most nutritious food options. I eat an avocado a day to help curve nutrient deficiencies because it is such a complete food source. If you've never had one, or don't like them try one with cold pressed olive oil and sea or pink Himalayan salt. It is my favorite food combination. Herbs are so beneficial for the human body. Taking herbs on a daily basis ensure optimum health and help to curb viruses, fungus, and bacteria that are trying to take over the human body. There are thousands to choose from! I love herbs!

    Like I said I am a raw foodist but I don't expect everyone to jump on the bandwagon and I'm not here to sell you on it, but I am going to thoroughly explain the benefits. What I do recommend is that you start by eating cleaner foods for your sake as well as the planets. It is so simple. WHOLE FOODS! :) They make you feel wonderful because your body can actually recognize what it is, unlike gmo's which cause indigestion because they are not recognizable by the human body and loads of health problems. Start by eating whole foods then switch to all organic whole foods because they contain more nutrients and less toxins. If you want to feel even better try transitioning to a vegetarian diet then a vegan diet. If you want to have more energy than you've ever had in your life then all raw foods is the way to go. The only problem you can have with this lifestyle is not eating enough of the right kinds of foods your body needs. It is wonderful. Educate yourself thoroughly if this is your wish. It is good for you and just as beneficial for the earth. Another reason I am a raw vegan is because of how toxic the food supply is as well as the air we breathe. If there's one thing that is actually ours, aside from our soul, it's our body. The fuel that we put in our mouths determine how much energy we have in addition to our mood. Our grandparents ate clean food but nowadays they call it organic. If I don't have access to what I want, or the wilderness to forage for wild food, then I'll still choose conventional produce over genetically modified processed food made from corn, wheat, and/or soy.

  Next, I want to talk about what we should eat, in addition to what you should never eat. However, you should always please your body by eating what you want when you want it, but it's best to plan ahead by surrounding yourself with healthy food. If you take supplements make sure they are sourced from plants and/or organic whole foods made without chemicals. The most conductive foods are living which in turn allow us to transmit more powerful frequencies. These are the only foods we should be eating because they are healthiest for our body and planet. Fruits and vegetables are the only living foods; in addition to a higher nutritional content than other food they contain digestive enzymes. Plants are the only food sources that contain these vital components to nutrition. Our body also produces these digestive enzymes, but I figure it is a waste of energy to eat something that doesn't digest itself. Never eat anything but whole foods because they are what nature provides for us and they are the most nourishing for our bodies. The healthiest food is organic because is made without the use of toxic chemicals.

    Aside from conventional meat genetically modified foods are some of the most toxic because the genes of crops are engineered to resist man made chemical pesticides and herbicides. DNA from insects are spliced into the food to help with pest control, and they have been genetically modifying animals such as salmon. GMOs have been proven to make us sterile, not to mention the list of adverse effects they have been proven to have on the human body such as various types of cancer and other diseases. Corn, soybeans, rapeseed (used to make canola oil), cotton, rice, papayas, zucchini, yellow squash,  pineapples, potatoes, salmon (yes salmon), sugar beets (which is what companies make conventional sugar out of), and almost all grains are the most commonly genetically modified foods. Also, there are many crops waiting on approval, but if you purchase organic it comes with a guarantee that it is not a genetically modified food. I believe bananas just got passed and will soon be on the market. If you want to check to see if a fruit or vegetable is genetically modified all you have to do is type the plu code from the sticker on it into google and it usually will always give you an answer.

    Almost all of the grains fed to conventional livestock are GMO, and they also used to feed these animals the dead sick animals which is how mad cow disease came about. A cow's natural diet is grass, not the grains they feed them now, which makes a huge difference in the concentration of omega 3 fatty acids and omega 6 fatty acids. Organic grass-fed animals contain high levels of omega 3s. Ideally experts are saying that you want a ratio of 1 to 1. The average American is not even getting close to this, while omega 6 being consumed in excess with the help of processed vegetable oils in processed foods, which causes development and learning issues. Like I said conventionally raised meat is probably the most toxic food you can be eating mainly because of the hormones and antibiotics they feed them which causes them to grow faster and weigh more before they are slaughtered. Studies have been proving that children have been developing earlier on in life because of these hormones they use in the production of these animals. Also, they live in very unnatural, unsterile conditions which cause them to produce a lot of stress hormones which transfer to us if we eat them. Also, I want to end on a note that anti means against, and biotic means life.

  Organic food or locally farmed produce, meat, and dairy are typically trustworthy and healthy, but I still recommend sourcing all your food. Some processed foods contain non-GMO verification on the package so it's best to look for these if you continue to eat these foods, but I do not advise eating any processed foods unless they're homemade from whole foods. Heavy metals, radiation, and fluoride are the common toxic culprits in the food and water that we need to consider when shopping. Any food or drink can be sent into a lab to check for toxicities and nutrition content. When I first started changing my diet to an all plant-based protocol, I kept a short grocery list in my wallet with a list of the non-organic produce containing the lowest levels of pesticides which is always updated online.

  Preservatives and artificial sweeteners used in processed foods are hard to detox from your body, inhibit your brain from transmitting frequencies, and often cause internal damage because they remain in the body if you continue to eat them without a detox protocol. Lemon juice, raw vinegars, and raw oils are the only healthy preservatives in my opinion. A whole foods diet is something everyone can do to stay healthy, happy, and GMO/preservative free. An easy way to get on a whole foods diet and stick to it is to start by replacing sugary junk foods with fruits, because let's face it we all get a sweet tooth sometimes. I believe our appetite for sugar is the hardest one to control. I recommend keeping lots of bananas in the house and allow them to ripen, and you know when they have plenty of brown spots. It is important to eat ripe fruits because they digest easier and they contain the most anticancer properties. Also it is important to eat fruits on an empty stomach or before meals instead of after because it will satisfy your craving for sweets and digest best. Fruit digests extremely fast and if there is food blocking it from digesting it will create acid and indigestion so it's best to eat dessert first! Some processed sugar is derived from genetically modified sugar beets grown with synthetic chemicals that have been proven detrimental to our health. Other healthy alternatives to conventional sugar include coconut sugar, lucuma, raw honey, or herbs such as stevia or lo han guo which contain no sugar.

    If you are going to cook I recommend using coconut oil because it is the most stable fat when heated. I don't eat any food that is cooked by means of stovetop or drink any water that has been boiled because when ingested both stimulate a response from our white blood cells (which is a part of our immune system). A good way to replace cooked food is to steam vegetables because this is the most efficient way to preserve the valuable components in food. When I make tea water I heat it at the lowest temperature possible until it is warm. I live primarily on liquids such as teas, fresh juices, and smoothies. Raw food is the better than most diets because you're not destroying the nutrients by cooking. I grew up on any food that was in front of me but by the time I was twenty I started just eating just whole foods. Now I only eat raw foods such as fruit, sprouts, vegetables, herbs, soaked nuts and seeds. I also enjoy raw fermented foods and drinks such as kombucha which are excellent for digestive health because they provide our body with a healthy dose of beneficial bacteria that aid with digestion. I'm not writing this book to preach veganism but I am going to give you my last two reasons to more eat plants. Animals that eat meat have very short digestive tracts which are basically straight through their body. Ours are on average between thirty and forty feet. My point is that parasites get into our body through undercooked meat that has been sitting around because most people do not eat it fresh. Besides this, parasites can help us to clear rotten meat out of our bodies which isn't bad, but some will feed off your tissues as well and the waste they leave behind is detrimental to our health, specifically the brain.

    I believe it to be very beneficial to be consuming, or preferably drinking herbs everyday. The best way to go about this is by experimenting until you find at least one or more that work best for you. If you're taking prescription medications prescribed by a doctor, it's best to consult with him or her first to help prevent any possible reactions. Herbs have been used for tens of thousands of years as medicine to help our bodies heal. They strengthen our immune system to help fight invaders such as bad bacteria, parasites, viruses, or even macro organisms which are visible to the naked eye! Chaga and Reishi mushrooms are two that I highly recommend because they greatly improve your immune system. Either can be taken as a tea, extract, supplement, or edible powder. They are great to jump start the detox process and I suggest to incorporate herbs in your diet every day to improve your well-being.

    Another tip regarding food I have found very helpful is to stop eating before 6 or 7 p.m. at the latest which helps with proper digestion, sleep patterns, and nutrient assimilation. Sip slow and chew slower.

## Fasting

This may sound odd to some but fasting has been one of the greatest experiences of my life. The longest recorded fast was three hundred and eighty two days in nineteen seventy one by a twenty seven year old male. Granted he was given some nutrients through intravenous methods and was supervised by doctors, but although I do not recommend this it goes to show that we don't need to eat nearly as much as we do. There have been many people that I know people that have water fasted for one week all the way up to ninety days. I enjoy fasting for twenty four hours, sometimes longer, at least one day a month.

The awesome fact is that science has proven it to be one of the most efficient ways to detoxify and regenerate the human body. There are fasting clinics all over the world which have helped people cure themselves from many illnesses. Although fasting is very effective and efficient at removing toxins from the body, the benefits go far beyond the physical aspects. Fasting helps with past traumas by allowing you the choice to let go as they resurface rather cover them up with means of stimulation such as food. It can also help you relive and reshape emotions and it gives you the opportunity to reconnect with the authentic spiritual self.

There are many reasons to fast on occasion or as often as you like. It rebuilds our bodies by helping our immune system and organs catch up because you give your body a break from food as well as everyday toxicities. We all have undigested fats, carbs, and proteins that need to be broken down. Fasting gives the body a rest and allows it to rejuvenate and heal in many ways. Most of us are overfed in addition to undernourished in today's society because of conventional farming. Animals fast all the time, especially when they are sick or injured. It allows your body to clean itself up by expelling built up toxins. There are many ways you can go about this through means of water, juice fasting, or intermittent. I fast when my body tells me to do so or when I want to clear my mind which it works wonders for.

## Toxins

The ecosystem fellow man has created for one another is being proven to be detrimental to the health of our bodies. Anything that is ingested through means of air, food, or water that is manmade, will be treated as a toxin within the body. Toxicity is the number one reason root to why we all don't physically feel as good as we should; furthermore lessening toxicities within the body and environment improves and lengthens our time here on this planet in countless ways. One way is that we are able to think clearer and transmit stronger frequencies due to the fact that our bodies are not using as much energy to rid themselves of toxins. The main toxins to avoid include: aluminum from deodorant or other sources like cans, fluoride, chlorine, genetically modified food, non-organic food, processed food, and cooked food, plastic, most prescription drugs, and alcohol. The sources to some of the most toxic substances we use on a daily basis include fluoride toothpaste, laundry, and dish soaps. I suggest using natural clay soaps for hand washing, and an environmentally friendly dish and laundry soap. Baking soda and apple cider vinegar are the two healthiest choices to replace shampoo and conditioner. Believe it or not but the toilet seat has been proven to be flawed for use with the human body because it restricts full potential elimination, which is why I use a stool in front of my toilet. When your feet are up in a squatting position it allows more waste to be dispelled from your body. This in turn will allow less parasites, bad bacteria, and toxins to accumulate in your colon. If you have mercury fillings I suggest that they be removed because mercury is a well-known neurotoxin. If you still get vaccinations I highly recommend that you research more into the matter because I have not found them to be harmful to your health.

    If you haven't already come to the realization that nearly every conventional product is toxic and disrupting to the body's hormone producing systems then I'm here to help you become aware of this. There are natural products that you can buy or make at home as I do. I love you use Google to find homemade non-toxic recipes. Making your own is not only cheaper, but way healthier! Baking soda, coconut oil, essential oils for scent, shea butter, vinegars, along with vodka all work wonders in whatever combination your heart desires for deodorants, dish soap, laundry detergent, toothpaste, and any self or home cleansing remedies you might need. Lastly, if you live in a city then I want to recommend a shower dechlorinator. Chlorine is great for the treatment of pathogens but it is toxic to the human. When it reacts with hot water in your shower it creates a gas that is breathed into the lungs causing the body to absorb it. You can purchase a high quality one for less than fifty dollars at freedrinkingwater.com. They also have reliable reverse osmosis water systems.

    After doing all the research, I've become aware to the sad truth that nearly everything, aside from organic and homegrown food, is polluted that we eat or drink which is why I started to grow my own produce. Don't worry though because there are countless ways to clean up our planet. We can all start by recycling and using less plastic so this landfill business can stop. Fungus is the most efficient way to rid our soils of chemicals from conventional farming, plastics, or other accumulated toxins. The more seeds, especially trees, we plant the cleaner our air will become. If you live in a cold climate, it is less expensive, warmer, drier, and less harmful for our planet if you use wood as the source to heat your home. Not to mention it makes you stronger!

    Now I'm going to talk about the materials in the clothes we all wear when we're in public, unless you are a part of a tribe that doesn't wear clothes then please disregard this bit. Many are petroleum based and have been known to contribute to toxicity related diseases. Organic clothing is the best choice for you and the planet but it's best to at least stick to cotton, hemp, wool, or any other natural fibers. Polyester or other synthetic based clothes are not good for your body or the environment.

    The bottom line is that we all have unlimited power and are very much in control of our own lives. I feel that the less toxins in your body, the better you will feel. Once you master your thoughts I do not believe anything can you back from achieving full potential and your deepest desires. The more you learn to love yourself, then the more you will be at peace. We all need to do our part to take care of our planet because after all without somewhere to live what place could we call our home. Constantly strive to please your body and may God bless your soul! The following methods are effective ways to help detoxify your body and come back into harmony and balance.

     Grounding is immensely life prolonging for the human body and incredibly simple as well as free. Grounding or earthing is a wonderful way to revitalize the entire system. There is a book entitled *Earthing: The most important health discovery ever?* which I highly recommended because it explains the scientific details and health benefits of this practice more in depth. It has helped numerous individuals heal from all sorts of health ailments. I'm actually standing on a grounding mat right now as I type this at my makeshift standing stand desk. The basic concept is that the earth is surrounded by a field of electrons that our body actually absorbs when we reconnect with it. If you want to invest some money to be grounded more often you can purchase a grounding device at earthing.com for when you sleep. I have one and I can honestly say that it has also been one of the best investments of my life because of the more restful sleep I get. Grounding or earthing is barefoot contact with the earth or a grounding device, which reconnects your body to the electron field that surrounds our planet. Grounding is probably the next best thing, besides changing your diet that helps your body detox to make you feel better. It's simple and it's free because all you have to do is walk barefoot on the earth. The electricity the earth provides us is so healing for our bodies. Earthing recharges your cells with electrons, allowing them to communicate, which allows your body to be more efficient at removing toxicity. Not only this, but it resets the electrical current of your brain, heart, other organs allowing them to function more optimal. Barefoot walks, runs, or sprints in the sun are the best way to feel better right now! The atmosphere is positively charged and when we put on shoes we greatly increase our chances of disease. Grounding has been shown to greatly decrease inflammation and oxidation, thus increasing our longevity. The following conditions have been known to improve when grounding: sleep troubles, pain, high blood pressure, allergies, asthma, sprains, strains, and more. When we set foot on the earth all of our bodily systems become rebalanced and our cells are able to communicate with each other thus allowing the body to remove toxicity easier. Also, when we are grounded we are not affected as much by frequencies from cell phones, Wi-Fi, microwaves and radar that throw off our body chemistry and can actually make us severely sick if we are constantly being bombarded in say, an office building. Like I said I sleep on a grounding device and I recommend that everyone invest in one; but until then just simply take a barefoot walk whenever possible. Other ways to improve your quality of sleep include, complete darkness, no TV before bed, and unplugging all your electronic devices which are giving off EMFs. You can also purchase EMF diffusers which help keep your body from harm's way of these invisible energies that cause harm to your body. EMFs damage your cells and prevent them from communicating as they go about their day to day activities. In my opinion, there is no right or wrong way to sleep. I'm a firm believer that you should sleep for as little or as long as your body signals for you to do so, whenever you desire! The human body sleeps in cycles of 90 minutes so it can help to base your patterns off this information.

    Who knew that sun exposure can help with detoxification, mind, and body rejuvenation? Without it the planet would not be inhabitable and we would not even be able to live here so I figure as much sun exposure as possible the better. The sun provides us with food and our bodies with energy. Exposure to it works synergistically with the skin to produce vitamin D, which is actually classified as a hormone.

Hormones create our behaviors and moods. The benefits of sun exposure are being more documented as the days go on but it has been known to cure depression and eliminate harmful bacteria from the body. Aim for at least thirty minutes a day but you should spend as much time in the sun as you are able to. Increasing your exposure can greatly improve your overall well-being and longevity. If you eat plenty of antioxidants from whole foods then you get all the protection you need from the harmful rays. Also, the sun positively affects our body and mood in a plethora of ways. The largest organ of the human body, which is our skin, uses the sun's rays to produce necessary hormones. Another key role of sunlight is that it triggers the production of serotonin, which is a chemical that brings us a feeling of well-being. I believe it is crucial to at least watch the sunrise and sunset in order receive some of the beneficial rays if not more when your body is ready to handle more sunshine. After all, without the sun our entire planet would cease to exist.

    The last three practices for detoxification I want to discuss are exercise, hot/cold therapy, ways to stimulate the lymphatic system, and grounding. The first is basically a form of exercise, which I suggest the most and so does NASA, is rebounding. Like cold showers along with inverting, they all flush toxins out of the lymphatic system with is a major part of the waste disposal system of the body. Rebounding is simply jumping on a trampoline! The best times to be aware of your breathing are during exercise, inverting, mediation, and yoga. I invert daily by means of headstands, but it can be accomplished easier with an inversion table which can be purchased. If you are not capable of headstands, handstands, or unable to purchase an inversion table then you can lean your body over the armrest of a couch or bed. It also stimulates the lymphatic system which is waste removal pathway of the body. It brings more blood to the brain and makes you feel great! Doing this for ten minutes counterbalances a whole day's worth of the harmful effects of gravity. Remember to breathe when you are inverting because it is so rejuvenating for your lungs. The more conscious of your breathing you become the more control you will have control over your thoughts, and in turn your life. A little bit of exercise goes a long way. You don't need to overwork your body at the gym to be in peak physical condition. Simply moving more and walking can be the best exercise protocol. Aside from breathing exercising is one of the most effective ways to boost your metabolism, burn unwanted belly fat, and remove toxins from the body. Hot/cold therapy has been proven to be one of the best forms of cellular exercise available because it pumps the lymph and releases an abundance of feel-good neurotransmitters. All you have to do is take a cold shower! You will feel fantastic! Some people like to go back and forth from hot and cold. I start and end my showers on cold, and honestly I love it. It is great for your skin because it tightens up your pores. Try it today!

    I have found that taking regular long walks on daily basis, yoga, and moderate exercise such as pushups, planks, squats, and sit ups keep my body in peak physical condition. Walking in the morning, before you eat breakfast, is a great start to lose weight, get healthier, and detoxify your body because right when you wake up your body is in the peak stage of detoxification. So if you wait an hour or two before eating you will extend and intensify the detox and fat burning mechanisms of your body.

    Before I end with a with final summary I want to leave you with a list of foods, nutrients, and products provided wholly from nature that will help with the detox and remineralization process. Health is wealth!

- Organic Whole Foods
- Activated Coconut Charcoal
- Aloe Vera
- Avocados
- Bee Pollen
- Bentonite Clay
- Berries (Organic and/or Wild)
- B-Vitamin Complex
- Chia Seeds
- Coffee (Organic and preferably shade grown)
- Chlorella
- Digestive Enzymes
- Essential Fatty Acids
- Fulvic Acid
- Green Vegetables and Herbs (The more the merrier!)
- Hemp Seeds
- Iodine (Mineral)
- Maca
- Magnesium (Mineral)
- Marine Phytoplankton
- Medicinal Mushrooms (Especially Chaga and Reishi)
- MSM
- Olive Oil (Cold pressed)
- Probiotics and/or Fermented Foods
- Raw Cacao (Chocolate)
- Sea Vegetables
- Silica (Mineral)
- Shilajit
- Spirulina

- Wild Foods
- Zeolite Clay

## Summary

- affirmations
- you are the creator of your reality
- you have the power to change your thoughts
- your thoughts determine the way you look and feel
- **Breathe to live and live to breath!**
- let go of doubtful thoughts
- stay in the moment as much as possible
- become conscious of your breathing
- **We all can be millionaires!**
- look at life through your peripherals
- be the experiencer
- love the experience
- love your body

Made in the USA
Columbia, SC
09 January 2019